OUR LIVING WORLD

Mammals

By **Jenny Tesar**

With Illustrations by Robert Clement Kray

Series Editor: Vincent Marteka

Introduction by John Behler, *New York Zoological Society*

A BLACKBIRCH PRESS BOOK

WOODBRIDGE, CONNECTICUT

Published by Blackbirch Press, Inc.
One Bradley Road, Suite 205
Woodbridge, CT 06525

©1993 Blackbirch Press, Inc.
First Edition

Printed in Canada

10 9 8 7 6 5 4 3 2 1

Editorial Director: Bruce Glassman
Editor: Geraldine C. Fox
Editorial Assistant: Michelle Spinelli
Design Director: Sonja Kalter
Production: Sandra Burr, Rudy Raccio

Library of Congress Cataloging-in-Publication Data

Tesar, Jenny E.
    Mammals / by Jenny Tesar.—1st ed.
        p.   cm. — (Our living world)
    Includes bibliographical references and index.
    Summary: Examines the physical structure, metabolism, and life cycle of mammals and discusses how they fit into the food chain.
    ISBN 1-56711-042-8   ISBN 1-56711-055-X (Trade)
    1. Mammals—Juvenile literature. [1. Mammals.] I. Title. II. Series.
QL706.2.T47   1993
599—dc20   92-44036
                                                                       CIP
                                                                        AC

Contents

What Does It Mean to Be "Alive"?

Introduction by John Behler,
New York Zoological Society

One summer morning, as I was walking through a beautiful field, I was inspired to think about what it really means to be "alive." Part of the answer, I came to realize, was right in front of my eyes.

The meadow was ablaze with color, packed with wildflowers at the height of their blooming season. A multitude of insects, warmed by the sun's early-morning rays, began to stir. Painted turtles sunned themselves on an old mossy log in a nearby pond. A pair of wood ducks whistled a call as they flew overhead, resting near a shagbark hickory on the other side of the pond.

As I wandered through this unspoiled habitat, I paused at a patch of milkweed to look for monarch-butterfly caterpillars, which depend on the milkweed's leaves for food. Indeed, the caterpillars were there, munching away. Soon these larvae would spin their cocoons, emerge as beautiful orange-and-black butterflies, and begin a fantastic 1,500-mile (2,400-kilometer) migration to wintering grounds in Mexico. It took biologists nearly one hundred years to unravel the life history of these butterflies. Watching them in the milkweed patch made me wonder how much more there is to know about these insects and all the other living organisms in just that one meadow.

The patterns of the natural world have often been likened to a spider's web, and for good reason. All life on Earth is interconnected in an elegant yet surprisingly simple design, and each living thing is an essential part of that design. To understand biology and the functions of living things, biologists have spent a lot of time looking at the differences among organisms. But in order to understand the very nature of living things, we must first understand what they have in common.

The butterfly larvae and the milkweed—and all animals and plants, for that matter—are made up of the same basic elements. These elements are obtained, used, and eliminated by every living thing in a series of chemical activities called metabolism.

Every molecule of every living tissue must contain carbon. During photosynthesis, green plants take in carbon dioxide from the atmosphere. Within their chlorophyll-filled leaves, in the presence of sunlight, the carbon dioxide is combined with water to form sugar—nature's most basic food. Animals need carbon, too. To grow and function, animals must eat plants or other animals that have fed on plants in order to obtain carbon. When plants and animals die, bacteria and fungi help to break down their tissues. This allows the carbon in plants and animals to be recycled. Indeed, the carbon in your body—and everyone else's body—may once have been inside a dinosaur, a giant redwood, or a monarch butterfly!

All life also needs nitrogen. Nitrogen is an essential component of protoplasm, the complex of chemicals that makes up living cells. Animals acquire nitrogen in the same manner as they acquire carbon dioxide: by eating plants or other animals that have eaten plants. Plants, however, must rely on nitrogen-fixing bacteria in the soil to absorb nitrogen from the atmosphere and convert it into proteins. These proteins are then absorbed from the soil by plant roots.

Living things start life as a single cell. The process by which cells grow and reproduce to become a specific organism— whether the organism is an oak tree or a whale—is controlled by two basic substances called deoxyribonucleic acid (DNA) and ribonucleic acid (RNA). These two chemicals are the building blocks of genes that determine how an organism looks, grows, and functions. Each organism has a unique pattern of DNA and RNA in its genes. This pattern determines all the characteristics of a living thing. Each species passes its unique pattern from generation to generation. Over many billions of years, a process involving genetic mutation and natural selection has allowed species to adapt to a constantly changing environment by evolving—changing genetic patterns. The living creatures we know today are the results of these adaptations.

Reproduction and growth are important to every species, since these are the processes by which new members of a species are created. If a species cannot reproduce and adapt, or if it cannot reproduce fast enough to replace those members that die, it will become extinct (no longer exist).

In recent years, biologists have learned a great deal about how living things function. But there is still much to learn about nature. With high-technology equipment and new information, exciting discoveries are being made every day. New insights and theories quickly make many biology textbooks obsolete. One thing, however, will forever remain certain: As living things, we share an amazing number of characteristics with other forms of life. As animals, our survival depends upon the food and functions provided by other animals and plants. As humans—who can understand the similarities and interdependence among living things—we cannot help but feel connected to the natural world, and we cannot forget our responsibility to protect it. It is only through looking at, and understanding, the rest of the natural world that we can truly appreciate what it means to be "alive."

1

Mammals: The Overview

Many of the animals you know best are mammals. Dogs, cats, horses, tigers, and elephants are mammals. So are baboons, whales, mice, and kangaroos. And you are a mammal, too!

Mammals live all over the world. Camels live in hot deserts, polar bears live in the icy Arctic. Giraffes live in grasslands, deer live in forests. Seals live in oceans, hippopotamuses spend a lot of time in rivers. Bats fly through the air, squirrels live in treetops, sheep graze on the ground, moles tunnel underground. There are mammals in every environment.

Each kind of mammal has certain adaptations that enable it to survive in its environment. A spider monkey has a long tail for holding on to branches high above the jungle floor. A dolphin is shaped like a torpedo, which helps it swim quickly through water. A camel has wide feet for walking on sand.

Opposite:
A black rhinoceros looks out across the African grasslands. Mammals live in every environment on Earth and include more than 4,000 species.

The Variety of Mammals

Scientists have identified more than 4,000 kinds, or species, of mammals. The largest mammal is the blue whale. It's the largest, heaviest animal that has ever lived. A blue whale may be 100 feet (31 meters) long and weigh 260,000 pounds (118,000 kilograms). Even whale babies are huge. A newborn blue whale may be 14 feet (4 meters) long and may weigh more than 14,000 pounds (6,350 kilograms).

The largest mammal that lives on land is the African elephant. It may be more than 11 feet (3 meters) tall and weigh 14,500 pounds (6,577 kilograms). If an elephant sat on one side of a seesaw, about 125 people your weight would have to sit on the other side to balance the seesaw!

The blue whale is the largest and heaviest mammal that has ever lived. It may reach 100 feet (31 meters) in length and may weigh up to 260,000 pounds (118,000 kilograms).

The smallest mammal is the shrew. The pygmy shrew of North America is 2 inches (5 centimeters) long from the tip of its nose to the base of its tail. It weighs only 4/5 ounce (23 grams), which is less than a dime weighs!

The tallest mammal is the giraffe. Some giraffes stand 17 feet (5 meters) tall. One third of this height is neck. Even though the neck is very long, it contains only seven bones—the exact same number of bones found in the human neck.

Speed is important to many mammals. They use bursts of speed to catch food—or to escape from being food for other animals. The fastest four-legged animal is the cheetah. This large cat may reach a speed of 70 miles (113 kilometers) an hour over

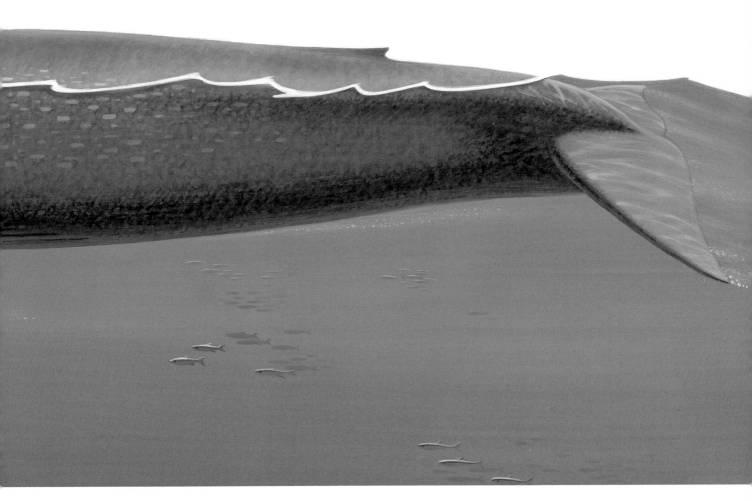

Speed is important to many mammals. The fastest four-legged mammal is the cheetah, which can reach speeds of up to 70 miles (113 kilometers) an hour.

short distances. Some bats can fly at speeds up to 35 miles (56 kilometers) an hour, and blue whales have been clocked swimming at up to 23 miles (37 kilometers) an hour. In contrast, the fastest humans run at speeds of about 15 miles (24 kilometers) an hour. The real slowpoke among mammals is the three-toed sloth, which lives in trees in South American rain forests. At top speed, the sloth moves only about 15 feet (5 meters) a minute—that's less than 1/5 mile (.32 kilometer) an hour.

Mammal Features

Mammals come in many shapes and sizes. Different species live in different places and have different behaviors. All of them, however, share a number of important features.

Backbones All mammals are vertebrates. That means they all have backbones. You can feel your backbone when you move your hand up and down the center of your back. You can also feel the backbone of a cat, for example, by moving your hand along the center of its back. The backbone consists of a series of bones called vertebrae. Other bones and many muscles are attached to the backbone.

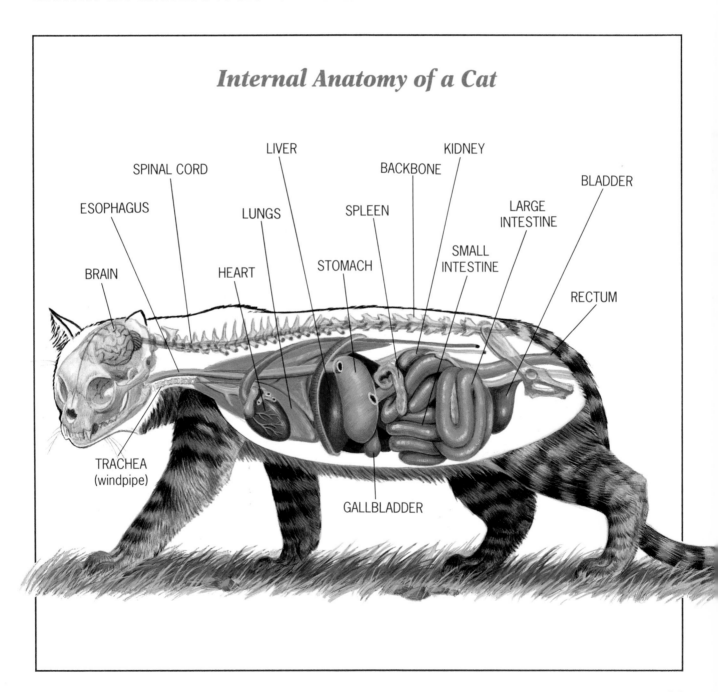

Internal Anatomy of a Cat

LIVER

KIDNEY

SPINAL CORD

BACKBONE

BLADDER

ESOPHAGUS

LUNGS

SPLEEN

LARGE INTESTINE

BRAIN

HEART

STOMACH

SMALL INTESTINE

RECTUM

TRACHEA (windpipe)

GALLBLADDER

Fish, reptiles, amphibians, and birds also are vertebrates. All other kinds of animals are invertebrates. An invertebrate has no backbone. A vertebrate's bony skeleton supports and shapes an animal's body. It works with the muscles to allow movement. It also protects the soft internal organs that can be easily punctured or bruised. For example, the skull protects the brain, and the ribs protect the lungs. Still another function of the skeleton is to manufacture blood cells. Blood cells are made in bone marrow—a soft, fatty material in the center of large bones.

Two pairs of limbs Like many other vertebrates, mammals have two pairs of limbs. The limbs are adapted for different functions, depending on the mammal and how it lives. An antelope has four long legs adapted for walking and running. A badger's limbs are adapted for burrowing into the ground. A squirrel monkey's arms are adapted for hanging from tall trees. The sea lion's limbs are flippers designed for swimming. Whales have only one visible pair of limbs. Whales descended from mammals that lived on land about 60 million years ago. Gradually, the whales' ancestors evolved, or changed. They developed special characteristics that enabled them to survive better in the sea. The whale's front legs evolved into flippers, and the back legs disappeared. But within a whale's body there are still some small leg bones that remain—reminders of the whale's ancient physical history.

Warm-bloodedness Mammals and birds are the only endothermic, or warm-blooded animals. Their body temperature remains almost the same all the time. A healthy armadillo's temperature is about 89.6 degrees F. (32 degrees C.). A healthy human's temperature averages 98.2 degrees F. (37 degrees C.). A healthy dog's temperature is about 101.5 degrees F.

Mammal Limbs: Two Pairs for Every Animal

ANTELOPE
(front legs and rear legs)

APE
(arms and legs)

BAT
(wings and feet)

SEA LION
(front flippers and
rear flippers)

BADGER
(front legs and
rear legs)

(38.6 degrees C.). In contrast, most exothermic (cold-blooded) animals have the same temperature as their surroundings. Warm-bloodedness allows mammals and birds to live in particularly harsh places where many other animals can't survive. A polar bear doesn't have to worry about meeting a rattlesnake on its journey across the Arctic ice!

Mammals and birds are the only animals that have four-chambered hearts. Mammals also have lungs to breathe in air. Even mammals that live in the water breathe air. A whale can dive deep into the sea and stay underwater for an hour or more. But it must return to the surface to take in air; otherwise, it will drown.

Mammary glands Mammals have some unique characteristics. Only mammals have mammary glands—from which their name came. The name comes from the Latin word *mamma*, which means "breast." The mammary glands, which are located in the body of female mammals, produce milk. Female mammals nurse their young with this milk.

Hair Mammals also are the only living animals that have true hair, or fur. Most mammals are covered

Mammals are the only animals that have mammary glands. Mammals got their name from the Latin word *mamma*, which means "breast." The mammary glands produce milk, which allows female mammals to breast-feed their young.

with a thick coat of hair. Hair insulates the body. It helps to keep the body temperature constant. Most mammals shed some of their hair in the warm weather. When the cold weather returns, they grow long, thick coats to keep warm.

Hair also serves a number of other purposes. Eyelashes keep sand out of a camel's eyes. Hairs in the human nose trap dust and keep it out of the lungs. Whiskers help a cat find its way at night. Sharp quills— which are hard, hairlike structures—protect a porcupine against predators.

Some mammals do not have much hair. A human has hair only in patches. An armadillo has just a few coarse hairs called bristles. Whales have only a few stubby hairs around the mouth. But whales need good insulation to keep warm in icy oceans. Under their skin they have a thick, insulating layer of fat called blubber.

The Mammal Brain

The most important difference between mammals and other animals is found in the brain. Mammals have the most highly developed brain. The part of the mammal brain that is especially well developed is the cerebrum. The cerebrum regulates the movement of hundreds of muscles in a mammal's body. It is also the center of intelligence, memory, and judgment.

Because of their highly developed brain, mammals are the most intelligent animals on Earth. And the most intelligent of all the mammals are humans. The extraordinary cerebrum of humans has enabled them to develop written and spoken languages.

Whales and elephants have the largest brains. An elephant brain weighs about 11 pounds (5 kilograms). A whale brain may be even heavier. A human brain weighs about 3 pounds (1 kilogram). Why, then, are humans the most intelligent? Intelligence seems to be related not to the size of a mammal's brain but to the amount of surface area in the cerebrum and its size relative to that of the entire body. The surface of the human cerebrum has many deep folds. This increases surface area, which in turn increases the total number of nerve cells in the surface layer of the cerebrum. The greater the number of these nerve cells, the greater the animal's intelligence. The surface layer of a human cerebrum contains more than two billion nerve cells!

Past, Present, and Future

Mammals have lived on Earth for more than 210 million years. That isn't very long when compared with other kinds of animals. Jellyfish have existed for more than 600 million years. The first fish appeared about 450 million years ago. The earliest reptiles appeared more than 300 million years ago.

The very first mammals developed, or evolved, from certain kinds of reptiles. These mammals were small, rather like today's moles and shrews. Over millions of years, different types of mammals developed. Because they were warm-blooded and could withstand changes in climate, they could adapt to changes in the environment.

The saber-toothed tiger, which lived millions of years ago, became extinct because it could not adapt quickly enough to changes in its environment.

Many kinds of mammals that lived long ago no longer exist. They died out, or became extinct. We know these mammals existed because researchers have found fossils. Fossils are remains or traces of living things that have been preserved in rocks, ice, and other materials.

Mammals—like all other living things—are still evolving. Evolution is a very, very slow process. But the evolution of a species can end

An Ancient Horse

MODERN HORSE

EOHIPPUS

Many of today's mammals look very different from their ancestors. The earliest known horse was a little animal called Eohippus, which means "dawn horse." Eohippus lived 50 million years ago. It was just a little bigger than a house cat—about 11 inches (28 centimeters) tall. It had a short neck and short legs. There were four toes on each front foot and three toes on each back foot. It had small teeth designed for eating leaves, and it lived in forests.

Gradually, over many millions of years, the descendants of Eohippus grew larger. Their necks and legs became longer. Their teeth changed. The modern horse evolved about 2 million years ago. It is about 5 feet (2 meters) tall—bigger than any of its ancestors. It has a long neck and long legs. There is only one toe on each foot, and the nail of each toe forms a hoof. The teeth are large and designed for eating grass. Today's horse lives on grasslands instead of in forests.

abruptly if the environment changes and the species cannot adapt to the changes fast enough. Woolly mammoths and saber-toothed tigers became extinct for this reason.

Rats and mice are plentiful throughout the world because they are extremely adaptable. They can live in a wide variety of habitats, and they can eat a wide variety of food.

Giant pandas are not as adaptable as rats and mice. These pandas are adapted to life in bamboo forests. They cannot live in other habitats. Their diet consists almost entirely of bamboo leaves. People have destroyed many of the bamboo forests where pandas once lived. Very few giant pandas remain on Earth. Will the species survive? Or become extinct, like woolly mammoths and saber-toothed tigers?

2

The Senses: How Mammals React

Have you ever watched a squirrel that is feeding in a park? It seems to be aware of everything that's happening around it. At the slightest disturbance, it sits up. Its eyes dart back and forth. If a squirrel senses danger, it races to the nearest tree and climbs up the trunk until it feels safe.

Perhaps you have seen a squirrel burying a nut. Squirrels save nuts for winter, when food is scarce. Will it find the nut again in months to come? Maybe. It's more likely that another squirrel will find the nut. Squirrels do not remember where they bury nuts, but a squirrel's sense of smell is so good that it can find a nut buried under a foot (.30 meter) or more of snow.

A mammal's eyes, nose, and other sense organs are constantly at work, gathering information about the environment. Any change in the environment that can be detected by a mammal's sense organs is

Opposite:
A red squirrel nibbles on a nut in the forest. Squirrels don't remember where they bury nuts and seeds, but their sense of smell can lead them to food that is under a foot (.30 meter) of snow.

called a stimulus. To stay alive, every living thing must be able to react to stimuli. The reaction that an organism makes to a stimulus is called a response.

Usually, a certain kind of stimulus causes a certain response. For example, a squirrel responds to an approaching cat by running away. This means that the information picked up by the squirrel's eyes has to be passed to its legs. This job is handled by the squirrel's nervous system. The nervous system is a system of communication and control. It coordinates all the squirrel's activities and reactions to stimuli.

The central parts of a mammal's nervous system are the brain and spinal cord. The brain is in the head, within the hard bone of the skull. The spinal cord runs from the brain down the back of the mammal, inside the backbone. A network of nerves extends from the brain and spinal cord to every part of the body. Nerves carry information in only one direction. One group of nerves may carry information from the eyes to the brain, telling the brain, for example, that the air is dusty. Another group of nerves, carrying information from the brain to eye muscles, will cause the eyes to blink.

What happens when a squirrel sees a cat? Nerve cells in the squirrel's eyes carry signals to fibers called sensory nerves. These sensory nerves connect to the brain, where the signals are passed down the spinal cord to motor nerves. The motor nerves run out to the leg muscles. They cause a muscular response to the stimulus. All this takes only a fraction of a second.

How Mammals See

A mammal's eye is like a camera. Near the front of the eye is a transparent lens. Light passes through the lens and is focused on a special surface. This surface is the retina (in a camera, it's a piece of film). Cells in

The Senses: How Mammals React

the retina send nerve impulses to the brain, which interprets the information gathered by the eye. Some mammals, including monkeys and humans, have cells on the retina that detect color. But most mammals see the world in black, gray, and white.

Every mammal has two eyes. In many mammals, including cattle and other plant-eaters, there is one eye on each side of the head. This gives a mammal a wide field of vision, which is useful for detecting predators. Other mammals, including monkeys and humans, have eyes in the front of the head. This arrangement allows both eyes to see the same object at the same time. This is called binocular vision. The result is a single image that is three-dimensional. A three-dimensional image is seen with depth, or placement in space. Binocular vision doesn't cover a very wide field of vision, but it enables animals to judge distances accurately.

Some mammals have spectacular vision. Most meat-eating mammals, such as cats, wolves, and foxes, have excellent eyesight used for spotting the movement of prey. Antelopes and other grazing animals generally have excellent eyesight as well. Burrowing mammals—those that live underground, such as moles and gophers—have relatively poor eyesight; they rely much more on touch to receive information about their environment.

Placement of the eyes on the head determines what kind of vision a mammal will have. Monkeys and humans have both eyes on the front of the head, giving them the ability to see objects in three-dimensional space. Camels and other plant-eaters have an eye on each side of the head, which gives them a wide field of vision.

How Mammals Hear

A typical mammal's ear has three regions: the outer ear, the middle ear, and the inner ear. The outer ear is the part of a mammal's ear that you can see. It catches sound waves and transmits them to the eardrum in the

I'm All Ears: The Incredible Elephant

African Elephant

The largest mammalian ears belong to the African elephant. An African elephant's ears may weigh more than 100 pounds (45 kilograms) each! In addition to enabling the elephant to hear, the large ears serve a second function. They allow the elephant to lose excess heat on hot days. If the elephant is too hot, blood vessels in its ears enlarge. Heat then passes out of the blood and skin into the air.

Sometimes, animals that are very similar have different ears because they have adapted to living in very different environments. The fennec fox, a desert fox, has very big ears that help it get rid of excess heat. Its relative, the arctic fox, has small ears. In the cold Arctic, big ears are a disadvantage. An arctic animal needs to conserve as much body heat as it can.

middle ear. Sound waves vibrate the eardrum. The vibrations pass through bones in the middle ear and go to the inner ear. The inner ear contains nerve endings that then carry impulses to the brain.

Cats have an excellent sense of hearing. So do dogs, rabbits, and hares. These animals can raise

The Senses: How Mammals React

their ears and turn them easily from side to side. This helps these animals to quickly locate the source or direction of a sound. Cats, dogs, rabbits, and hares are much more dependent on their sense of sound for survival than are humans.

Whales do not have outer ears—they disappeared as the whales evolved (just as their back legs disappeared). But whales do have middle and inner ears. They have exceptionally good hearing. They detect sounds that travel through water. They depend on hearing to find food, sense depths, sense the presence of objects in water, and communicate with one another. Moles and some other burrowing animals that do not have well-developed outer ears can detect sounds that travel through the ground.

Many animals can hear sounds that humans cannot hear. For example, a "silent" dog whistle makes high-pitched sounds that dogs can hear but that are above the range of human hearing. Humans are also unable to hear most of the sounds made by mice. But a cat can hear these sounds.

Many mammals, such as the antelope jackrabbit, rely heavily on their ability to hear in order to survive. Jackrabbits—like cats, dogs, and hares—have excellent hearing because they can raise their ears and rotate them toward the source of a sound.

Bats use echolocation to navigate in the dark and to find food. While flying through the air, bats make high-pitched sounds that bounce off nearby objects and return to their highly sensitive ears as echoes.

Echolocation

Bats depend on sound to find their way at night and to find food. They use a system called echolocation. As a bat flies through the air, it makes very high-pitched sounds at the rate of 30 to 100 sounds per second. The sounds reflect from objects in the bat's path. They bounce back as echoes, which are heard by the bat's very sensitive ears. Different objects create different echoes. By

The Senses: How Mammals React

interpreting the echoes, a bat can judge the size, location, and speed of an object. The bat's echolocation system is so good that it can easily find a flying mosquito—or avoid flying into a thin wire.

Bats aren't the only mammals that echolocate. Dolphins use echolocation to find food and other objects in the water. And scientists have certain evidence suggesting that shrews use echolocation.

The Sense of Smell

A mammal's smell cells are inside its nose. These cells detect chemicals in the air. Nerves connected to the cells carry this information to the olfactory (smell) center of the brain.

There are about 10 million smell cells in the human nose. They make it possible for you to detect a wide variety of odors. But compared with many other mammals, humans have a poor sense of smell. Many mammals have a much more highly developed sense of smell. Deer depend heavily on their noses to detect danger. Dogs use their noses to track prey. Beavers use their noses to find poplars and other food trees. Many mother mammals can recognize their babies by their smell.

Scent glands Most mammals have special scent glands that produce smelly secretions. The location and purpose of these glands vary from species to species. Coyotes have scent glands between the toes and at the base of the tail. Deer have scent glands near their eyes, on their legs, and between their toes. Skunks have scent glands near the base of the tail.

Some animals, including cats, use scent to mark their territory. When your cat rubs its cheek on your leg, it is rubbing scent-gland secretions on you. The secretions are putting the cat's scent on you. This marks you and tells other cats about your cat.

Skunks are masters at using scent for defense. If a skunk is threatened, it can spray a foul-smelling oil on its potential attacker from as far away as 9 feet (3 meters).

Heaven Scent: Using the Nose

Some noses aren't just for smelling. The star-nosed mole has 22 fleshy feelers on its nose that help the little animal feel its way through underground tunnels. The large nose of a male proboscis monkey swells when the monkey calls, which makes the calls very loud. Some bats have leaf-shaped appendages on their noses. These help to focus sounds made by the bats as they fly through the air—much like a flashlight focuses a beam of light.

The world's biggest nose belongs to the elephant. It's the elephant's trunk. It may be 10 feet (3 meters) long. Smell is an elephant's most important sense. But the trunk has many other uses. An elephant uses flexible "fingers" on the tip of its trunk to rub its eye or to pick up small objects such as a blade of grass or a peanut. It uses the trunk to suck up water, which it then squirts into the mouth. It uses the trunk to spray dust and mud on its back, which helps protect it against biting insects. An elephant also uses the trunk as a trumpet, to magnify screams, grunts, and other sounds.

Male proboscis monkey

Reindeer and other animals that live in herds use scent to keep their groups together. Reindeer have scent glands between their toes. Secretions from the glands serve as trail markings for the herd.

Skunks are masters at using scent for defense. If a predator approaches a skunk, the skunk raises its tail and stomps its feet. If this doesn't scare away the predator, the skunk sprays an awful-smelling oily liquid—and its aim is excellent. A skunk can hit a predator's face from a distance of 9 feet (3 meters)!

Taste, Touch, and Balance

A rich variety of valuable information is also gathered by other sense organs. A ring-tailed lemur may lick another lemur's muzzle to get a taste of what it is

Stink Fight

Male ring-tailed lemurs have glands on their arms that produce a very smelly secretion. A male uses this secretion to mark his territory. He rubs it on trees and other objects in the territory. This tells other male ring-tails, "Keep Out!"

If another male enters the territory, the two lemurs engage in a stink fight. Each male rubs some of the smelly secretion on his tail. Then one lemur faces the other lemur, raises his tail, and flicks the secretion at his rival.

eating. Prairie dogs "kiss" to identify members of their group. Walruses use their highly sensitive whiskers to find crabs and clams on the ocean bottom.

Taste Like smell, taste is a chemical sense. The organs of taste, called taste buds, are spread out over the surface of a mammal's tongue. They detect chemicals that are dissolved in water or saliva.

Touch A mammal's skin contains sense organs that detect touch and pressure. These organs are not evenly distributed over an animal's body. Think of your hands, for example. Your fingertips are more sensitive to touch than are the backs of your hands. That is because the skin of your fingertips is more densely packed with sense organs.

One animal with an excellent sense of touch is the mole. It depends on its sense of touch to find its way underground and to locate earthworms, beetles, and other prey.

Balance Structures in the inner ear play an important role in maintaining balance—and also in telling a mammal which way is up or down when its eyes are closed. When a mammal's head changes position, sensory cells in the inner ear detect the movement and alert the brain. The brain can then make adjustments throughout the body to maintain balance.

The Senses: How Mammals React

Prairie dogs use touch and smell in a unique way. When prairie dogs meet, they "kiss" each other to identify members of their group.

The Senses: How Mammals React

Metabolism:
How Mammals Function

In Africa, a zebra races across a flat plain, hoping to outrun a lion. In North America, a moose walks slowly through a forest. In Australia, a spiny anteater explores an anthill. In Europe, a noctule bat flies high into the air, then swoops down to grab a beetle. In Asia, a human turns out the bedroom light and goes to sleep. In South America, a llama leaps across rocks high in the Andes Mountains. All over the world, mice scurry through people's houses, looking for food.

Mammals, like all other living things, need energy to survive. They need energy to walk, run, fly, and swim. They need energy to eat, fight, grow, and reproduce. They even need energy to sleep.

Mammals get the energy they need from food. Obtaining food, digesting it, and then breaking it down for energy is a complex process involving many chemical reactions. Together, these reactions—plus

Opposite:
An Australian koala chews on leaves from a eucalyptus tree. In order to survive, mammals—like all other living things—get the energy they need from food.

all the other chemical activities that take place in a mammal's body—are called metabolism.

Metabolism marks the major difference between a living organism and a lifeless object, such as a stone. Every living thing carries out metabolism. When metabolism stops, an organism dies.

Because they are warm-blooded, mammals have a high rate of metabolism. This means they must eat large amounts of food to supply the energy needed to keep their body temperatures high. For the chemical process needed to break down the food for energy, mammals need oxygen. They breathe in oxygen through their lungs. In the process of producing energy, mammals create wastes. These wastes must be removed, or excreted, from the body.

What Mammals Eat

Mammals eat a very wide variety of things. Some mammals, such as zebras and moose, eat only plants. They are called herbivores. Other mammals, such as lions and killer whales, eat only animals. They are called carnivores. Mammals that eat both plants and animals are omnivores. Bears, raccoons, rats, and humans are a few common omnivores.

Some mammals eat many different kinds of foods. A California ground squirrel eats leaves, flowers, roots, seeds, fruits, insects, bird eggs, young birds, and small reptiles. Other mammals have specialized diets. Koalas eat only the leaves of certain kinds of eucalyptus trees.

Different teeth for different diets Teeth are used to grab food and to break it down into smaller pieces. Chewing prepares food for digestion as saliva begins to break food down. The chemicals of digestion can mix with, and react with, food more easily when the food is in small pieces.

Season the Dinner

Often, a mammal's diet changes with the seasons. Many mammals take advantage of foods that are available only at certain times of the year. The grizzly bear of Alaska eats roots in the spring. In early summer it eats reed grass and horsetails. In late summer it feeds on berries and on salmon that swim up river to lay their eggs. During all seasons, the bear catches and eats ground squirrels.

Metabolism: How Mammals Function

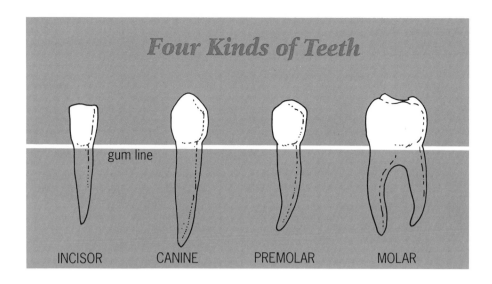

Four Kinds of Teeth

gum line

INCISOR   CANINE   PREMOLAR   MOLAR

There are four main kinds of teeth: incisors, canines, premolars, and molars. Each kind does a different job. Humans have all four kinds, but this is not true for all mammals. Incisors are the teeth in the front of your mouth—four in the upper jaw and four in the lower jaw. On each side of the incisors is a long, pointy canine tooth. Next come the premolars and, finally, the molars.

By looking at a mammal's teeth, you can learn about its diet. Lions and many other meat-eaters have long, sharp canine teeth designed for stabbing prey. Their premolars have sharp edges for cutting flesh into pieces.

Some mammals, like the moose, are herbivores. This means that they eat only plants.

A walrus's tusks are really just two very long and very strong canine teeth. They are especially designed for digging up clams, mollusks, and other animals that dwell in the sand on the bottom of the ocean.

Walrus tusks are actually very long—and very strong—canines. These tusks are designed especially for digging up clams and other mollusks from the ocean bottom.

Grazing mammals, such as horses, have sharp chisel-shaped front teeth. These are adapted for catching hold of grass and breaking it off. A horse's molars have broad, flat surfaces for grinding.

A rodent's front teeth are also shaped like chisels. However, they grow continuously throughout the rodent's life. For example, a beaver uses its incisors to gnaw tree trunks. This activity wears down the teeth. But because the teeth keep growing, they remain a constant length.

Lips and tongues are also adapted for special diets. A manatee, which lives in rivers and bays, grazes on underwater plants. The manatee's upper lip has two wide lobes that hang down and partly cover the lower lip. The two lobes are used to grasp and pull apart plants. Heavy bristles around the lips help push plants into the manatee's mouth.

The manatee, which grazes on underwater plants, has two wide lobes on its upper lip that help it to grasp and pull apart plants.

Most mammals need water to live. The kangaroo rat, however, never drinks any water at all. It gets all the water it needs from eating grasses and juicy cacti.

The giant anteater has no teeth at all. It eats only ants and termites, which it picks up with its long and sticky tongue. Another mammal with no teeth is the blue whale. This giant whale has long, thin plates of a comb-like material called baleen—set very close together all around the upper jaw. In feeding, the whale opens its mouth and takes in a huge gulp of water that is filled with tiny crustaceans called krill. The whale then closes its mouth. It forces water out between the baleen plates. The krill are trapped by fringes on the inner edges of the plates. The whale licks off the krill and swallows them.

Water Water is an important part of every mammal's diet—and an important part of its body. A human that weighs 100 pounds (45 kilograms) is about 70 pounds (32 kilograms) of just plain water!

An elephant may drink 40 gallons (151 liters) of water in one day. That's equal to 640 eight-ounce glasses! At the other extreme is the kangaroo rat, which lives in deserts in western North America. It never drinks any water at all. It gets water from grasses and the juicy pulp of cacti. When only dry seeds are available, the kangaroo rat gets all the water it needs by metabolizing sugar in the seeds.

Digesting Food

Before the body of a living thing can use food, the food has to be broken down into simple chemicals. The process of breaking down food is called digestion.

Cud-ly Ruminants: Chewing Food Twice

Because they eat different kinds of foods, mammals have interesting variations in their digestive systems. Meat-eaters have shorter digestive tubes than do plant-eaters. Plant food is bulkier. It is also harder to digest.

Some grass-eating mammals are known as ruminants. They include cows, goats, giraffes, antelope, camels, and deer. A ruminant stomach has four compartments. When a ruminant eats, it gathers grass rapidly. It chews the grass only slightly before swallowing. When it finishes feeding, it finds a quiet place to ruminate, or chew, its food for a second time.

When a ruminant first swallows its food, the food enters the first two compartments of the stomach. Here, bacteria break down the food to a pulp. (This is especially useful for animals like the giraffe, which often eat tough twigs and leaves.) A small mass of the pulp, called cud, is brought back into the mouth. The animal chews the cud, then swallows it again. The cud passes through the other compartments of the stomach, where digestion then continues.

Giraffes on the African plains

Chewing first breaks down the food into tiny pieces; then the pieces are broken down chemically.

A mammal's digestive system is basically a tube that begins with the mouth. From the mouth, food passes down the esophagus into the stomach. Then it enters the small intestine, where digestion is completed. The digested food particles plus water then pass through the wall of the small intestine and go into the blood. The blood carries the food particles to all the cells of the body. Any undigested materials are stored in the large intestine as waste. They are eventually pushed to the end of the digestive tube so they can leave the body through the anus.

Various glands connect to the digestive tube. These glands produce chemicals that help digest food. For example, salivary glands secrete saliva into the mouth. Saliva moistens the food and makes it easier to swallow. Saliva also contains a chemical that helps the body to digest starch. Other glands, such as the liver and the pancreas, secrete digestive chemicals into the stomach and small intestine.

Getting Oxygen

Each cell in the body of a living thing needs energy to function properly. Cells get this energy from food. To release energy from food, oxygen is needed. A fish takes oxygen from water. An insect takes oxygen from the air. A mammal has two lungs that absorb oxygen from the air. The oxygen passes into the

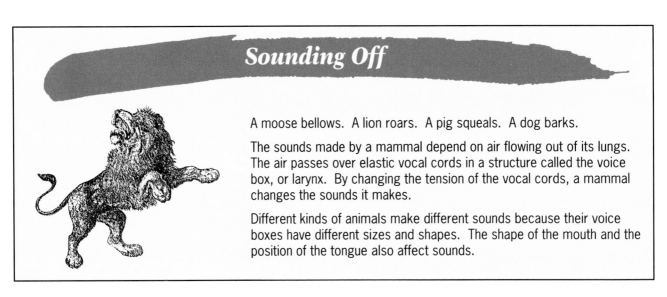

Sounding Off

A moose bellows. A lion roars. A pig squeals. A dog barks.

The sounds made by a mammal depend on air flowing out of its lungs. The air passes over elastic vocal cords in a structure called the voice box, or larynx. By changing the tension of the vocal cords, a mammal changes the sounds it makes.

Different kinds of animals make different sounds because their voice boxes have different sizes and shapes. The shape of the mouth and the position of the tongue also affect sounds.

How the Diaphragm Works

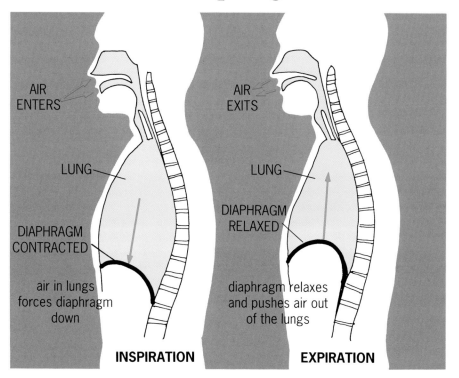

AIR ENTERS

LUNG

DIAPHRAGM CONTRACTED

air in lungs forces diaphragm down

INSPIRATION

AIR EXITS

LUNG

DIAPHRAGM RELAXED

diaphragm relaxes and pushes air out of the lungs

EXPIRATION

During inspiration, or breathing in, the dome-shaped diaphragm contracts and moves downward. The ribs move outward, and air enters the lungs. During expiration, or breathing out, the diaphragm relaxes and expands upward. The ribs move inward, forcing the lungs to empty.

blood, which carries it to the cells. There, the oxygen is used by the cells to break apart food molecules and release energy.

Unlike all other animals, mammals have a special muscle called a diaphragm. The diaphragm helps the lungs to work and makes breathing more efficient. The diaphragm is a large sheet-like muscle that separates the chest from the abdomen. The chest contains the lungs and the heart. The abdomen contains the stomach, the intestines, and other soft organs.

When the diaphragm contracts, it makes the chest cavity bigger. Air enters and fills the lungs, and the lungs spread out to fill the chest cavity. When the diaphragm relaxes, it makes the chest cavity smaller. Air is then pushed out of the lungs.

Metabolism: How Mammals Function

Removing Wastes

All mammals—indeed, all living things—produce wastes during metabolism. The process of removing wastes from the body is called excretion. One waste produced during metabolism is carbon dioxide gas. Mammals excrete carbon dioxide through their lungs when they exhale. Other wastes are excreted through the kidneys. The kidneys produce a liquid called urine, which flows out of the body through a tube called the urethra.

Mammal Blood

Blood moves materials throughout a mammal's body. About half the blood is a fluid called plasma. The other half of the blood is made up of solid materials, mostly blood cells. The red color comes from hemoglobin, a compound in red blood cells.

Functions of the blood Blood carries food and oxygen to the cells. It also has some other important functions. It carries carbon dioxide and other wastes away from the cells. It carries hormones, which help regulate various body processes. It carries substances that fight and destroy germs. And it helps to keep a mammal's body temperature constant.

A mammal's blood travels to all parts of the body through one-way streets called blood vessels. The blood is pushed through the vessels by the heart.

The four-chambered heart A mammal's heart is a pump made out of muscles. It has four rooms, or chambers. The top two chambers are called the atria (singular, "atrium"). The bottom two are called the ventricles. Each atrium connects to a ventricle below it by a heart valve. As the valve opens and closes, it controls blood flow from the atrium to the ventricle. Blood flows only from an atrium to the ventricle below it, never the other way.

Metabolism: How Mammals Function

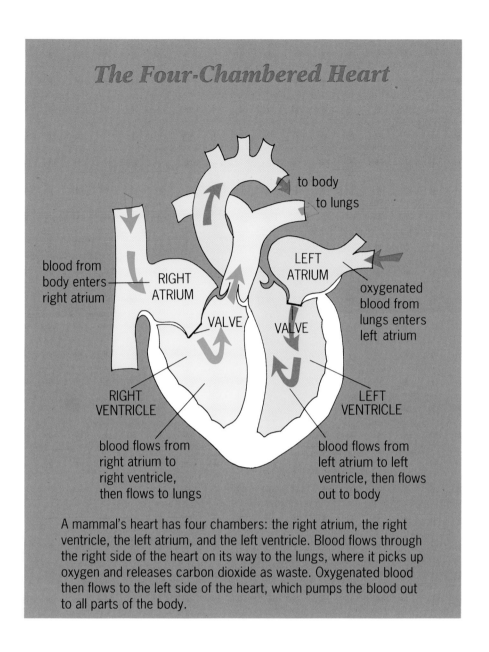

The Four-Chambered Heart

to body

to lungs

blood from body enters right atrium

RIGHT ATRIUM

LEFT ATRIUM

oxygenated blood from lungs enters left atrium

VALVE

VALVE

RIGHT VENTRICLE

LEFT VENTRICLE

blood flows from right atrium to right ventricle, then flows to lungs

blood flows from left atrium to left ventricle, then flows out to body

A mammal's heart has four chambers: the right atrium, the right ventricle, the left atrium, and the left ventricle. Blood flows through the right side of the heart on its way to the lungs, where it picks up oxygen and releases carbon dioxide as waste. Oxygenated blood then flows to the left side of the heart, which pumps the blood out to all parts of the body.

Blood flowing from a mammal's legs, stomach, brain, and other organs enters the right side of the heart, which pumps the blood to the lungs. In the lungs, the blood gets rid of carbon dioxide and picks up oxygen. Then it flows to the left side of the heart, which pumps the blood to the rest of the body.

The rate at which a heart pumps blood varies from animal to animal. It also varies within each animal, depending on the animal's age, health, and activity. When an adult human sits quietly, the heart beats about 70 times a minute. But during exercise it may beat up to 150 times a minute.

Reproduction and Growth

Reproducing—creating more members of a species—is one of the most important activities of living things. If the members of a species do not reproduce, the species dies out, or becomes extinct.

Reproduction means "making more of the same." Although wolves, bats, humans, dolphins, and other mammals look very different from one another, there are many similarities in how they reproduce.

Meeting a Mate

In most living things, reproduction requires a male and a female. For mammals, the first step in reproduction is finding a partner. Most female mammals have a definite breeding cycle. At a certain point in the cycle, the female is ready to mate. Her body usually signals her readiness by secreting chemicals called pheromones. Each species produces its own

Opposite:
Because reproduction creates more members of a species, it is one of the most important activities of any living thing. Most mammals take special care to raise their young, feeding, teaching, and protecting them.

A Breath of Fresh Air: Underwater Mammals

Hippopotamus

Whales are born underwater, but like all mammals, they must breathe air. As soon as a whale is born, its mother pushes it to the surface of the ocean for its first breath of air. Then, when it is ready to nurse, the mother lies on her side at the water's surface. This makes it possible for the baby whale to nurse and breathe at the same time.

Another mammal born underwater is the hippopotamus. It, too, must quickly get to the surface to breathe. After a baby hippo has filled its lungs with air, it sinks back to the bottom of the river or pool, where it can stay for up to five minutes. Then it has to return to the surface for another breath of air.

kind of pheromones. When a mature male smells pheromones given off by a female of the same species, he follows the scent until he reaches the female.

In some species, including bears and chipmunks, the two animals separate after mating and may never see each other again. In other species, the male and female stay together for one or more seasons. Foxes, for example, stay together for most of the year. Some mammals mate for life. Beavers and jackals remain together until one of the partners dies.

The Developing Embryo

Each parent has special sex organs. The male has organs called testes (or testicles), which produce sex cells called sperm. The female has organs called ovaries, which produce eggs. During mating, the male deposits sperm inside the female. When a sperm combines with an egg, fertilization occurs. Once an egg is fertilized, it contains all the material needed to produce a new member of the species.

A fertilized egg consists of only one cell. But this cell soon divides to form two cells. The two cells then divide to form four cells. This process is repeated over and over again. Soon there are hundreds, then thousands, then millions of cells.

The developing mammal is called an embryo. In three particular mammal species, called monotremes, the embryo develops in an egg laid by the mother. In all other mammals—called marsupial mammals and placental mammals—the embryo develops within the mother's body.

Egg-laying mammals The only monotremes, or egg-laying mammals, are the duck-billed platypus and two species of spiny anteaters. They live in Australia and on some of the nearby islands. After mating, the female lays eggs that have a tough leathery covering. Within each egg is an embryo.

A female platypus makes a nest of leaves in her burrow. She lays two round eggs in the nest. She curls around the eggs, guarding them and keeping them warm. During this time, she does not leave the burrow at all. The eggs hatch in about 10 days. A newborn platypus is very tiny and not fully developed. It will not be ready to leave the burrow until it is about four months old.

The duck-billed platypus is one of only three mammal species that lay eggs instead of developing an embryo inside their bodies. These species are called monotremes.

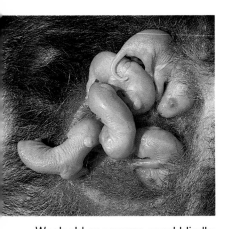

Week-old opossums crawl blindly around their mother's pouch. Opossums—like kangaroos and koalas—are marsupials, which means they incubate their young in pouches on their bellies.

A female spiny anteater develops a fold of skin on her belly during the breeding season. When she is ready to lay an egg, she rolls herself up in such a way that the egg falls into the pouch-like fold. The egg stays there for about 10 days. The heat of the mother's body keeps the egg warm. When the baby spiny anteater is ready to hatch, it uses a special tooth on the top of its snout to break the eggshell. This tooth has no other use, and it falls off soon after the baby hatches. The baby stays in the "pouch" for about two months before it begins to explore the outside world.

Marsupial mammals Kangaroos, koalas, and opossums are examples of marsupial mammals. The female usually has a pouch, or marsupium, on her belly. The embryos begin to develop inside the mother's body in an organ called the uterus. But the babies are born at a very early stage. They are blind, hairless, and not completely formed. A baby gray kangaroo weighs only .03 ounce (.85 gram) at birth. It's hardly bigger than a bumblebee!

At birth, tiny marsupial babies use claws on their front feet to crawl into their mother's pouch. The babies remain in the pouch until development is complete. A baby gray kangaroo doesn't leave the pouch until it is about 11 months old.

Placental mammals In most mammals—called placental mammals—the embryo remains in the uterus for a comparatively long time. The baby is not born until it reaches an advanced stage of development. The embryo is connected to the uterus by a structure called the placenta. Within the placenta, the blood vessels of the mother and the embryo are very close together. Food and oxygen pass from the mother's blood to the embryo's blood. Carbon dioxide and other wastes pass from the embryo's blood back to the mother's blood.

Three Kinds of Mammal Reproduction

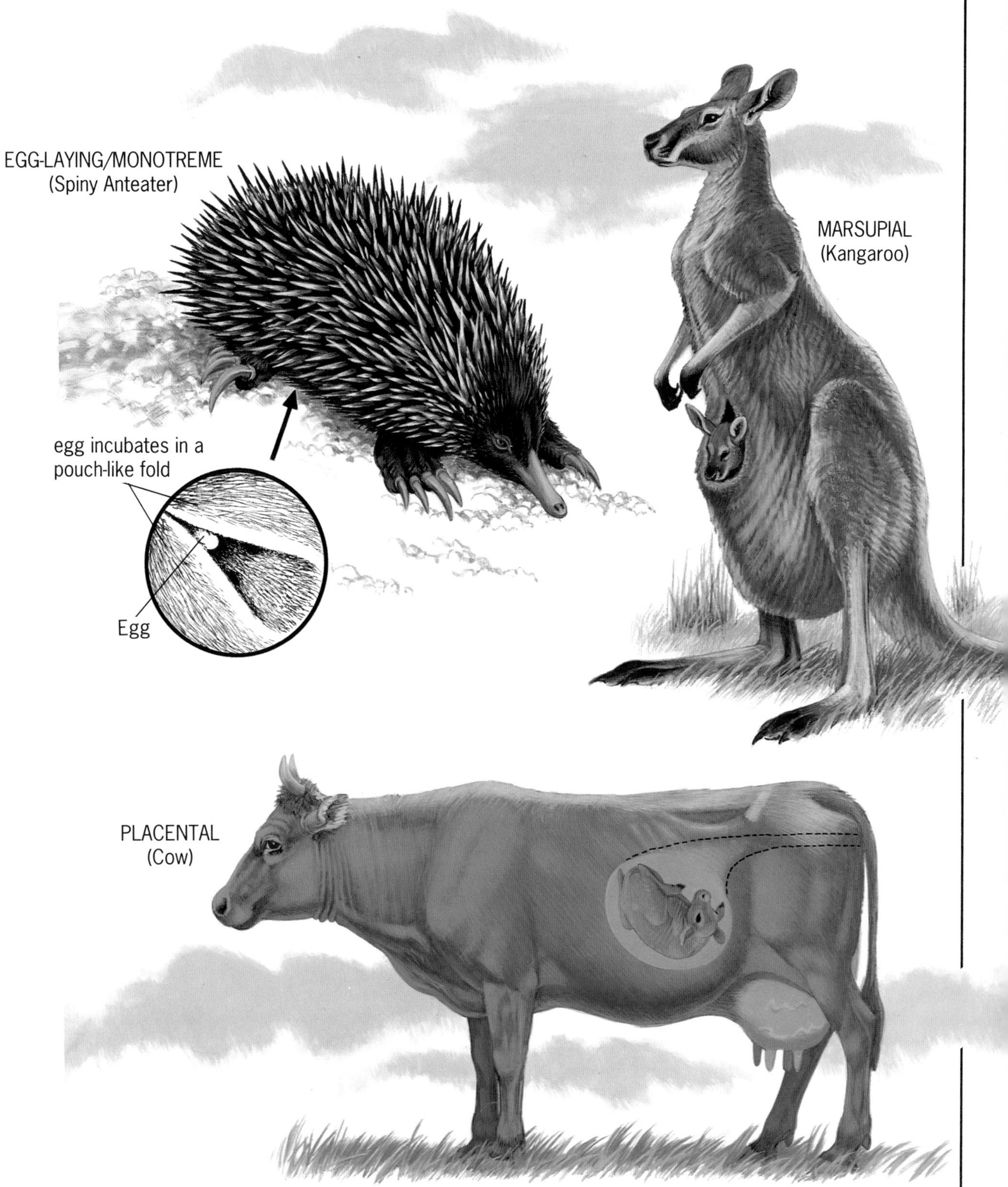

EGG-LAYING/MONOTREME
(Spiny Anteater)

MARSUPIAL
(Kangaroo)

egg incubates in a
pouch-like fold

Egg

PLACENTAL
(Cow)

The period from fertilization to birth is called the gestation period. In mice, the gestation period is 20 days. In lions, it's 108 days; in humans, 280 days; and in horses, 336 days. Elephants have the longest gestation period of all. A female elephant carries her embryo for about 640 days—almost 2 years!

Caring for the Young

Baby mammals get some of the best parent care in the animal world. Most often, they are cared for by their mothers—sometimes with help from their fathers—until they are almost fully grown.

Some mammals are practically helpless at birth. Kittens and puppies are born with their eyes closed. They can barely crawl. Human babies do not learn to walk until they are about a year old. But a baby zebra can stand when it is only 20 minutes old. It can walk only an hour after birth.

All baby mammals are fed milk, which is produced by the mother's mammary glands. The female doesn't produce milk all the time. Her mammary glands make milk only after she gives birth. The milk provides all the food her babies need. It contains protein, sugar, fat, vitamins, and minerals.

Long Live the Mammals: Life Spans

Gorilla

Under ideal conditions, a guinea pig may live to be 14 years old. A dog may live to the age of 29. And an elephant may reach the age of 78.

Each species has a certain life span—the length of time from birth until death. The size of a mammal usually is a clue to its life span. In general, the larger the mammal, the longer its life span. A tiny shrew, which weighs less than an ounce, has a life span of only 1 or 2 years. Commerson's dolphins, which weigh about 90 pounds (41 kilograms), have a life span of about 20 years.

Monkeys and other primates have longer life spans than other mammals of the same size. This may be a result of their greater intelligence. Savanna monkeys, which weigh 6 to 15 pounds (3 to 7 kilograms), have a life span of more than 30 years. The primates with the longest life span are humans. In fact, humans are the longest living of all mammals. The highest-known age ever reached by a human is 120 years!

Some mammals have milk that is rich in protein. Their babies grow very quickly. The milk of a dolphin mother contains 10 times more protein than that of a human. A baby dolphin doubles its birth weight in about 1.5 weeks. A human baby needs about 26 weeks to double its birth weight.

Some mammals, such as pigs, produce milk that is very rich in protein and their young rapidly increase their birth weight. Here, piglets nurse eagerly on their mother.

Babies of small mammals nurse (feed on their mothers' milk) for only a short time. Babies of large mammals nurse for longer periods. A kitten nurses for about eight weeks; an elephant nurses for two years or more. Gradually, the babies change over to the diet that is typical of the species. Kittens learn to eat meat. Baby elephants begin to eat leaves.

A mother introduces her babies to solid foods. In meat-eating species, such as cats, the mother catches and kills an animal for food before her babies know how to hunt and while they aren't strong enough or fast enough to chase and catch another animal on their own. When the babies are bigger, they begin to follow their mother and imitate her behavior on hunting trips.

Mammal parents also protect their young from danger. Many mammals hide their babies in burrows, caves, tall grass, and other places where predators do not see them. If baby mammals are discovered by a predator, their parents must act quickly to save them. Some mammal families try to run away from danger. But many times, parents will attack a predator. Deer and giraffes kick at anything that threatens their babies. Buffalo and mountain goats use their horns as daggers. Bears and lions attack with their sharp claws. Mammal parents often put their own lives in danger so their young may have a chance to live.

5

Fitting into the Web of Life

Every living thing must be able to survive in its own unique environment. How an organism looks, how its body works, and how it behaves are all connected to the kind of environment in which it must live. An organism's environment is made up of many elements, including the land, food sources, and other living things. In a healthy environment, all these elements create a balance for the many things that share a habitat.

Every mammal, like every other living thing, has evolved special characteristics that allow it to survive. Giraffes are among the best-known of all mammals. They live in Africa, in open grasslands dotted with scattered bushes and trees. A giraffe's favorite foods are the leaves and twigs of acacia trees. Its great height allows it to reach high into trees for food. A

As a rhinoceros moves through the African bush, it often carries a bird—or two or three birds—on its back. The birds are oxpeckers, or tick birds. Both the rhino and the oxpeckers benefit from this relationship.

The oxpeckers get their favorite foods. They eat ticks and insects that attach themselves to the rhino's skin. This rids the rhino of pests.

The oxpeckers are also good guards. If they spot danger, they warn the rhino by pecking on the rhino's head to make it hurry away.

Oxpeckers spend most of their lives on the backs of rhinos, warthogs, and other large mammals of the African plains. They often sleep and even mate on the mammals' backs.

giraffe is a big eater. It can eat more than 160 pounds (73 kilograms) of acacia leaves a day!

Giraffe eyes are very large, and their vision is very sharp. A giraffe can recognize other members of its herd at a distance of more than 1/2 mile (.80 kilometer). A giraffe can also spot danger quickly, using not only its eyes but also its excellent senses of smell and hearing. Giraffes will often graze with antelopes, zebras, and ostriches. This helps to protect the animals. As soon as one animal sees a predator, it alerts the others.

As they run away from a predator or brushfire, giraffes can reach speeds of as much as 35 miles (56 kilometers) an hour. If cornered, a giraffe kicks. A well-aimed kick can kill even a lion.

Without plants to eat and water to drink, a giraffe would soon die. Without the security of being part of a herd, it would be in greater danger. Like all living things, a giraffe does not live alone. It lives in an environment with many other living and non-living things. It depends on its environment for survival, and it has many adaptations that enable it to thrive in its surroundings. The giraffe's adaptations include its unique way of getting food, its sharp senses, its long neck, and its powerful legs.

Eating...and Being Eaten

In every environment, energy passes constantly from one organism to another by way of food. This transfer of energy is called a food chain. A food chain describes who eats whom or what. All food chains begin with green plants. Green plants make food. Mammals and other animals cannot make food. They must eat something. Some mammals, such as giraffes, feed on green plants. Other mammals, such as lions, eat animals that feed on the plants.

Most mammals eat a variety of foods; they are a part of many food chains. For example, a giraffe eats both the leaves of the acacia plant and the leaves of mimosa and wild apricot trees. It can also eat grass. A lion's diet consists of giraffes, antelopes, zebras, water buffalo, and other animals. Eating a variety of foods gives giraffes and lions a better chance to survive. If one food is missing from the environment, they can eat another.

A group of lions feasts on a freshly killed zebra. Most mammals eat a variety of foods and are part of a variety of food chains. Eating a mix of foods helps to increase a mammal's chances for survival by increasing its food options.

Mammals have many different adaptations to obtain food. The giraffe's long neck is very useful for reaching acacia leaves. The lion's powerful legs and sharp claws are adaptations for hunting.

Adapting to Changing Seasons

When the dry season comes to the African grasslands, herds of plant-eating mammals travel in search of green grass and water. Lions and other predators follow close behind. The regular movement of the animals is called migration.

Mammals usually migrate in search of food or warm weather. American elk spend the summer high in the mountains, feeding on herbs and grasses. As winter approaches, the elk descend to valleys, where there is better protection against icy storms. In winter, elk strip the bark of trees and eat it.

Some mammals migrate thousands of miles each year. California gray whales spend the winter in warm waters off the coast of southern California. In the spring, they swim north to spend the summer in the cold waters of the North Pacific.

Every living thing has some adaptations that enable it to better survive in its environment. The snowshoe hare is able to grow an entirely different coat of fur for the winter and the summer. During the summer (*below, left*), it has a brown coat that blends with the colors of the ground. In the winter (*below, right*), it grows a white coat that blends with the snow-covered surroundings.

Many mammals that do not migrate survive cold winters by hibernating in caves or by burrowing underground. During hibernation, body temperature drops, and heart and breathing rates slow down. Very little energy is needed by the body during this time. The energy is obtained by burning fat that the animal has built up during the previous summer and fall. Squirrels, chipmunks, bears, and marmots are examples of mammals that hibernate in winter.

Defense in the Natural World

Mammals have various adaptations that are designed to protect them against danger. Like giraffes, several mammals depend mainly on speed. Many have long legs powered by strong muscles.

Armadillos and porcupines are well protected by a kind of armor. The armadillo has many hard bony shields over its back and sides. When another animal threatens the armadillo, it curls up into a ball. In this position, the armadillo's soft underside is protected. Porcupines are covered with about 30,000 sharp spines called quills. The quills come out at the slightest touch, spearing any attacker.

Some mammals are colored to blend in with their surroundings. This is called camouflage. The snowshoe hare has a brown summer coat that blends into the arctic ground during warm weather. In fall, the hare sheds this coat and grows a white coat, which hides it as it moves over snow-covered ground during winter. Tiny green algae live in the fur of the three-toed sloth of South America. This gives the

Different mammals have evolved different means of defense. The porcupine (*below*) has approximately 30,000 spiny quills on its body that spear its enemies. The armadillo (*bottom*) has a tough armor-like shell that protects it from attackers when it curls into a ball.

fur a greenish color, which blends with the leaves of the trees among which the sloth lives.

If it has to, a mammal will fight to defend itself. Tigers use their sharp teeth and claws as weapons against enemies. Elephants can trample enemies or stab them with their tusks. Moose deliver powerful kicks, and howler monkeys, which live in tall trees in tropical forests, throw things. If howlers are threatened by a predator climbing up a tree in which they sit, they break off branches and drop them on the predator. Howlers may even excrete on an intruder!

The Human Connection to Mammals

Mammals are important to people in many ways. People raise cattle, sheep, pigs, and other hoofed mammals for meat, milk, and other dairy products. The skins of cattle, deer, and pigs are made into shoes, clothing, and bags. Large mammals like horses and water buffalo are used for transportation, farming, and hard labor. Cats, dogs, and guinea pigs are some of the most popular pets.

Insect-eating bats are valuable because they eat enormous quantities of pests. In only one hour a little

Some mammals are popular pets because they are able to form a close bond with humans and can share affection.

People feel a special connection to mammals because mammals are among the most intelligent animals on Earth.

A Hare-Raising Experience

In its natural home, a mammal lives in balance with other creatures. But if the mammal is introduced into a new home, it can cause a lot of trouble. It upsets the delicate balance that exists in the environment.

People have often introduced mammals into new homes. Sometimes, they have done this on purpose. Sometimes, they have done it accidentally.

In 1859, a man in Australia became homesick for the animals of his native England. He imported two dozen wild rabbits. In England, rabbits have many natural enemies. The enemies keep the rabbit population under control. But in Australia, rabbits have no natural enemies, so their numbers grew rapidly. Soon there were millions of rabbits. They spread out across much of Australia. They stripped fields of grass, turning large areas into wastelands.

Australians started a campaign to kill all the rabbits. A great deal of money was spent trying to rid the continent of rabbits. But for almost a century, these efforts were unsuccessful. Finally, in 1959, scientists introduced a special virus into Australia. The virus infected and killed most of the rabbits. But some rabbits were not harmed by the virus. They survived...and kept multiplying. Today, rabbits are still a problem in Australia.

brown bat can eat 600 mosquitoes! Armadillos also help control populations of unwanted insects.

Other mammals are pests to humans. Mice, rats, and rabbits eat crops and stored food. Mice and rats also carry the germs that cause such illnesses as plague, typhus, rabies, and Lyme disease.

People have made life very difficult for some mammals. As a result of human actions, a growing number of mammals face the threat of extinction. People have brought blue whales to the brink of extinction through overhunting. People have also endangered orangutans through destruction of the rain forests in which orangutans live. People have threatened the future of striped dolphins by polluting the seas in which dolphins swim.

It would be very sad if blue whales, orangutans, striped dolphins, and other threatened mammals became extinct. Once an animal is extinct, it is lost forever. It cannot be recreated.

Orangutans are among the many species of mammals that are threatened with extinction. Many animals are in danger as a result of harmful human activities.

Classification Chart of Mammals

Kingdom: Animal
Phylum: Chordata
Class: Mammalia

Scientists have identified more than 4,000 species of mammals. These species are classified in about 18 major living orders (different scientists use different classification systems).

Major Order	Common Members	Distinctive Features
Monotremata "one hole"	duck-billed platypuses, spiny anteaters	digestive and reproductive tracts open to the outside through the same hole; lay eggs
Marsupialia "pouched animals"	kangaroos, koalas, opossums, wombats	females usually with a pouch on the belly; young very immature at birth
Insectivora "insect-eaters"	moles, hedgehogs, shrews	small; eat insects
Edentata "without teeth"	sloths, anteaters	toothless or with reduced number of teeth
Chiroptera "hand wings"	bats	front limbs designed for flying
Carnivora "flesh-eaters"	cats, dogs, weasels	canines modified into fangs; mainly meat-eaters
Cetacea "whales"	seals, walruses, whales, dolphins, porpoises	water-dwelling mammals with fish-like forms
Tubulidentata "tube-toothed"	aardvarks	tubular mouth with slender, sticky tongue; feed on ants and termites

Major Order	Common Members	Distinctive Features
Proboscidea "in front, to feed"	elephants	huge mammals with trunks
Hyracoida "shrew mice"	hyraxes	rabbit-sized, with a hoof-like nail on each toe; eat plants and insects
Perissodactyla "odd number of toes"	horses, zebras, rhinoceroses, tapirs	hoofed mammals with an odd number of toes on each back foot; plant-eaters
Artiodactyla "even number of toes"	cows, goats, pigs, camels, deer, giraffes, bison	hoofed mammals with an even number of toes on each foot; plant-eaters
Rodentia "gnawers"	mice, rats, beavers, chipmunks, porcupines	gnawing mammals with two pairs of large chisel-shaped teeth that never stop growing
Pholidota "covered with scales"	pangolins	body covered by large, horned plates; no teeth; insect-eaters
Lagomorpha "hare forms"	rabbits, hares, pikas	small- to medium-sized plant-eaters with stubby or no tails
Sirenia "sirens"	sea cows, manatees, dugongs	aquatic; paddle-like front limbs, no back limbs; plant-eaters
Dermoptera "skin wings"	flying lemurs	one living species; wing-like membranes for gliding between trees
Primates "number one"	lemurs, monkeys, apes, humans	the most intelligent mammals; hands and feet designed for holding

Porifera SPONGES	Cnidaria COELENTERATES	Platyhelminthes FLATWORMS	Nematoda ROUNDWORMS	Mollusca MOLLUSKS	Annelida TRUE WORMS

Hydrozoa HYDRAS, HYDROIDS

Scyphozoa JELLYFISH

Anthozoa SEA ANEMONES, CORALS

Turbellaria FREE-LIVING FLATWORMS

Monogenea PARASITIC FLUKES

Trematoda PARASITIC FLUKES

Cestoda TAPEWORMS

Polyplacophora CHITONS

Gastropoda SNAILS, SLUGS

Bivalvia CLAMS, SCALLOPS MUSSELS

Cephalopoda OCTOPUSES, SQUID

Polychaeta MARINE WORMS

Oligochaeta EARTHWORMS, FRESHWATER WORMS

Hirudinea LEECHES

Biological Classification

The branch of biology that deals with classification is called taxonomy, or systematics. Biological classification is the arrangement of living organisms into categories. Biologists have created a universal system of classification that they can share with one another, no matter where they study or what language they speak. The categories in a classification chart are based on the natural similarities of the organisms. The similarities considered are the structure of the organism, the development (reproduction and growth), biochemical and physiological functions (metabolism and senses), and evolutionary history. Biologists classify living things to show relationships between different groups of organisms, both ancient and modern. Classification charts are also useful in tracing the evolutionary pathways along which present-day organisms have evolved.

Over the years, the classification process has been altered as new information has become accepted. A long time ago, biologists used a two-kingdom system of classification; every living thing was considered a member of either the plant kingdom or the animal kingdom. Today, many biologists use a five-kingdom system that includes plants, animals, monera (microbes), protista (protozoa and certain molds), and fungi (non-green plants). In every kingdom, however, the hierarchy of classification remains the same. In this chart, groupings go from the most general categories (at the top) down to groups that are more and more specific. The most general grouping is PHYLUM. The most specific is ORDER. To use the chart, you may want to find the familiar name of an organism in a CLASS or ORDER box and then trace its classification upward until you reach its PHYLUM.

Insecta INSECTS

Chilopoda CENTIPEDES

Diplopoda MILLIPEDES

Symphyla, Pauropoda SYMPHYLANS, PAUROPODS

Collembola, SPRINGTAILS
Thysanura, SILVERFISH, BRISTLETAILS
Ephemeroptera, MAYFLIES
Odonata, DRAGONFLIES, DAMSELFLIES
Isoptera, TERMITES
Orthoptera, LOCUSTS, CRICKETS, GRASSHOPPERS
Dictyptera, COCKROACHES, MANTIDS
Dermaptera, EARWIGS
Phasmida, STICK INSECTS, LEAF INSECTS
Psocoptera, BOOK LICE, BARK LICE
Diplura, SIMPLE INSECTS
Protura, TELSONTAILS
Plecoptera, STONEFLIES
Grylloblattodea, TINY MOUNTAIN INSECTS
Strepsiptera, TWISTED-WINGED STYLOPIDS
Trichoptera, CADDIS FLIES

Embioptera, WEBSPINNERS
Thysanoptera, THRIPS
Mecoptera, SCORPION FLIES
Zoraptera, RARE TROPICAL INSECTS
Hemiptera, TRUE BUGS
Anoplura, SUCKING LICE
Mallophaga, BITING LICE, BIRD LICE
Homoptera, WHITE FLIES, APHIDS, SCALE INSECTS, CICADAS
Coleoptera, BEETLES, WEEVILS
Neuroptera, ALDERFLIES, LACEWINGS, ANT LIONS, SNAKE FLIES, DOBSONFLIES
Hymenoptera, ANTS, BEES, WASPS
Siphonaptera, FLEAS
Diptera, TRUE FLIES, MOSQUITOES, GNATS
Lepidoptera, BUTTERFLIES, MOTHS

Insectivora, INSECTIVORES (e.g., shrews, moles, hedgehogs)
Chiroptera, BATS
Dermoptera, FLYING LEMURS
Edentata, ANTEATERS, SLOTHS, ARMADILLOS
Pholidota, PANGOLINS
Primates, PROSIMIANS (e.g., lemurs, tarsiers, monkeys, apes, humans)
Rodentia, RODENTS (e.g., squirrels, rats, beavers, mice, porcupines)
Lagomorpha, RABBITS, HARES, PIKAS
Cetacea, WHALES, DOLPHINS, PORPOISES

Carnivora, CARNIVORES (e.g., cats, dogs, weasels, bears, hyenas)
Pinnipedia, SEALS, SEA LIONS, WALRUSES
Tubulidentata, AARDVARKS
Hyracoidea, HYRAXES
Proboscidea, ELEPHANTS
Sirenia, SEA COWS (e.g., manatees, dugongs)
Perissodactyla, ODD-TOED HOOFED MAMMALS (e.g., horses, rhinoceroses, tapirs)
Artiodactyla, EVEN-TOED HOOFED MAMMALS (e.g., hogs, cattle, camels, hippopotamuses)

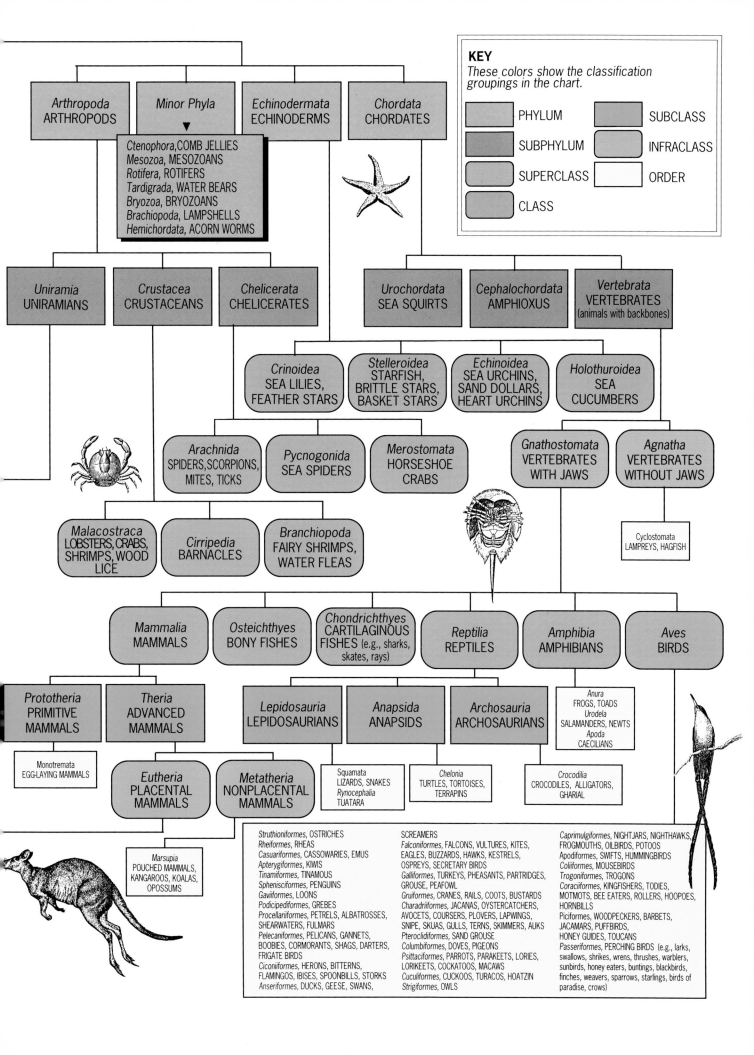

KEY

These colors show the classification groupings in the chart.

PHYLUM   SUBCLASS

SUBPHYLUM   INFRACLASS

SUPERCLASS   ORDER

CLASS

Arthropoda ARTHROPODS

Minor Phyla

Echinodermata ECHINODERMS

Chordata CHORDATES

Ctenophora, COMB JELLIES
Mesozoa, MESOZOANS
Rotifera, ROTIFERS
Tardigrada, WATER BEARS
Bryozoa, BRYOZOANS
Brachiopoda, LAMPSHELLS
Hemichordata, ACORN WORMS

Uniramia UNIRAMIANS

Crustacea CRUSTACEANS

Chelicerata CHELICERATES

Urochordata SEA SQUIRTS

Cephalochordata AMPHIOXUS

Vertebrata VERTEBRATES (animals with backbones)

Crinoidea SEA LILIES, FEATHER STARS

Stelleroidea STARFISH, BRITTLE STARS, BASKET STARS

Echinoidea SEA URCHINS, SAND DOLLARS, HEART URCHINS

Holothuroidea SEA CUCUMBERS

Arachnida SPIDERS, SCORPIONS, MITES, TICKS

Pycnogonida SEA SPIDERS

Merostomata HORSESHOE CRABS

Gnathostomata VERTEBRATES WITH JAWS

Agnatha VERTEBRATES WITHOUT JAWS

Malacostraca LOBSTERS, CRABS, SHRIMPS, WOOD LICE

Cirripedia BARNACLES

Branchiopoda FAIRY SHRIMPS, WATER FLEAS

Cyclostomata
LAMPREYS, HAGFISH

Mammalia MAMMALS

Osteichthyes BONY FISHES

Chondrichthyes CARTILAGINOUS FISHES (e.g., sharks, skates, rays)

Reptilia REPTILES

Amphibia AMPHIBIANS

Aves BIRDS

Prototheria PRIMITIVE MAMMALS

Theria ADVANCED MAMMALS

Lepidosauria LEPIDOSAURIANS

Anapsida ANAPSIDS

Archosauria ARCHOSAURIANS

Anura
FROGS, TOADS
Urodela
SALAMANDERS, NEWTS
Apoda
CAECILIANS

Monotremata
EGG-LAYING MAMMALS

Eutheria PLACENTAL MAMMALS

Metatheria NONPLACENTAL MAMMALS

Squamata
LIZARDS, SNAKES
Rynocephalia
TUATARA

Chelonia
TURTLES, TORTOISES, TERRAPINS

Crocodilia
CROCODILES, ALLIGATORS, GHARIAL

Marsupia
POUCHED MAMMALS, KANGAROOS, KOALAS, OPOSSUMS

Struthioniformes, OSTRICHES
Rheiformes, RHEAS
Casuariformes, CASSOWARIES, EMUS
Apterygiformes, KIWIS
Tinamiformes, TINAMOUS
Sphenisciformes, PENGUINS
Gaviiformes, LOONS
Podicipediformes, GREBES
Procellariiformes, PETRELS, ALBATROSSES, SHEARWATERS, FULMARS
Pelecaniformes, PELICANS, GANNETS, BOOBIES, CORMORANTS, SHAGS, DARTERS, FRIGATE BIRDS
Ciconiiformes, HERONS, BITTERNS, FLAMINGOS, IBISES, SPOONBILLS, STORKS
Anseriformes, DUCKS, GEESE, SWANS,

SCREAMERS
Falconiformes, FALCONS, VULTURES, KITES, EAGLES, BUZZARDS, HAWKS, KESTRELS, OSPREYS, SECRETARY BIRDS
Galliformes, TURKEYS, PHEASANTS, PARTRIDGES, GROUSE, PEAFOWL
Gruiformes, CRANES, RAILS, COOTS, BUSTARDS
Charadriiformes, JACANAS, OYSTERCATCHERS, AVOCETS, COURSERS, PLOVERS, LAPWINGS, SNIPE, SKUAS, GULLS, TERNS, SKIMMERS, AUKS
Pteroclidiformes, SAND GROUSE
Columbiformes, DOVES, PIGEONS
Psittaciformes, PARROTS, PARAKEETS, LORIES, LORIKEETS, COCKATOOS, MACAWS
Cuculiformes, CUCKOOS, TURACOS, HOATZIN
Strigiformes, OWLS

Caprimulgiformes, NIGHTJARS, NIGHTHAWKS, FROGMOUTHS, OILBIRDS, POTOOS
Apodiformes, SWIFTS, HUMMINGBIRDS
Coliiformes, MOUSEBIRDS
Trogoniformes, TROGONS
Coraciiformes, KINGFISHERS, TODIES, MOTMOTS, BEE EATERS, ROLLERS, HOOPOES, HORNBILLS
Piciformes, WOODPECKERS, BARBETS, JACAMARS, PUFFBIRDS, HONEY GUIDES, TOUCANS
Passeriformes, PERCHING BIRDS (e.g., larks, swallows, shrikes, wrens, thrushes, warblers, sunbirds, honey eaters, buntings, blackbirds, finches, weavers, sparrows, starlings, birds of paradise, crows)

Glossary

adaptation A body part or behavior that helps an organism survive in its environment.

appendage A body part attached to another body part.

atria The two top chambers of the heart, through which blood flows to the ventricles.

binocular vision Using both eyes to see in three dimensions.

bone marrow A soft, fatty material in the center of bones.

camouflage The colors, shapes, or structures that enable an organism to blend with its surroundings.

carnivore An animal that eats animals.

cerebrum The part of a mammal's brain that is the center for intelligence, memory, and judgment.

cud Partially digested food.

diaphragm A muscle between the chest and the abdomen that helps in breathing.

digestion The mechanical and chemical breakdown of food into substances the body can use for growth and energy.

echolocation A system of animal navigation that uses sounds and echoes.

embryo A young developing organism.

endothermic Warm-blooded.

esophagus The structure through which food passes from the mouth to the stomach.

evolution Change over a long period of time.

excretion The removal of bodily wastes.

exothermic Cold-blooded.

extinct No longer in existence.

fertilization The union of sperm and egg, which leads to the development of a new organism.

food chain The order in which organisms feed on one another in an ecosystem.

gestation period The time between the fertilization of an egg and the birth of a young mammal.

hemoglobin A compound in red blood cells that gives them their color.

herbivore An animal that eats only plants.

hibernation A seasonal period of rest when the body processes slow down.

hormones Chemicals that regulate body processes.

invertebrate An animal without a backbone.

lens A clear structure at the center of the eye through which light passes to the retina.

mammary gland A milk-producing organ in female mammals.

marsupial A mammal whose young develop in a pouch on the outside of the body.

metabolism The chemical processes in cells that are essential to life.

migration The seasonal movement of animals.

monotreme An egg-laying mammal.

olfactory Having to do with the sense of smell.

omnivore An animal that eats both plants and animals.

ovaries Female organs that produce eggs.

pheromones Chemicals secreted by female animals when they are ready to mate.

placenta The structure that connects the embryo to the uterus.

placental mammal A mammal whose young develop inside a mother's uterus attached to a placenta.

plasma The fluid part of blood.

predator An animal that kills other animals.

prey Animals that are eaten by other animals.

primates Members of the highest order in the animal kingdom; include humans and apes.

quills The sharp, spiny structures used by a porcupine for defense.

reproduction The process by which organisms create other members of their species.

retina A light-sensitive coating on the back of the eye, like the film of a camera.

ruminant A mammal that chews cud.

salivary gland An organ that secretes saliva into the mouth.

species A group of organisms that share many traits with one another and that can reproduce with one another.

stimuli Messages received by an animal's senses from its surroundings.

testes (testicles) Male sex organs.

urethra The tube through which urine passes out of the body.

urine Liquid waste from the kidneys.

uterus The female organ in which the embryo develops.

ventricles The two lower chambers of the heart that accept blood from the atria.

vertebrae The bones that make up the backbone.

vertebrate An animal with a backbone.

For Further Reading

Bailey, Jill. *Save the Tiger*. Milwaukee: Raintree Steck-Vaughn, 1990.

Bailey, Jill, and Seddon, Tony. *Animal Movement*. New York: Facts On File, 1988.

Bailey, Jill, and Seddon, Tony. *Animal Parenting*. New York: Facts On File, 1988.

Bailey, Jill, and Seddon, Tony. *Animal Vision*. New York: Facts On File, 1988.

Brooks, Bruce. *Nature by Design*. New York: Farrar, 1991.

Brooks, Bruce. *Predator*. New York: Farrar, 1991.

Cherfas, Jeremy. *Animal Defenses*. Minneapolis: Lerner Publications, 1991.

Cherfas, Jeremy. *Animal Societies*. Minneapolis: Lerner Publications, 1991.

Dow, Lesley. *Whales*. New York: Facts On File, 1990.

Gallant, Roy A. *The Rise of Mammals*. New York: Franklin Watts, 1986.

Gelman, Rita Golden. *Monkeys and Apes of the World*. New York: Franklin Watts, 1990.

Kerrod, Robin. *Primates, Insect Eaters and Baleen Whales*. New York: Facts On File, 1988.

Losito, Linda. *Mammals: Small Plant-Eaters*. New York: Facts On File, 1988.

Matthews, Rupert. *The Age of Mammals*. New York: Franklin Watts, 1990.

Minelli, Giuseppe. *Mammals*. New York: Facts On File, 1988.

Oram, Liz, and Baker, Robin. *Mammal Migration*. Milwaukee: Raintree Steck-Vaughn, 1992.

O'Toole, Christopher, and Stidworthy, John. *Mammals: The Hunters*. New York: Facts On File, 1988.

Parker, Steve. *Mammal* (Eyewitness Books). New York: Alfred A. Knopf, 1989.

Patent, Dorothy Hinshaw. *The Way of the Grizzly*. New York: Clarion, 1987.

Peisel, Michel, and Allen, Missy. *Dangerous Mammals*. New York: Chelsea House, 1992.

Smith, Roland. *Primates in the Zoo*. Brookfield, CT: The Millbrook Press, 1992.

Stefoff, Rebecca. *Extinction*. New York: Chelsea House, 1992.

Stidworthy, John. *Mammals: Large Plant-Eaters*. New York: Facts On File, 1988.

Index

African elephant, 22 (photo)
Anatomy
    external, 12–14, 13 (artwork)
    internal, 11 (artwork), 11–16
Antelope
    anatomy, 12, 13 (artwork)
    eating habits, 35, 50
    eye and vision, 21
Antelope jackrabbit, 23 (photo)
Arctic fox, 22
Armadillo, 12, 15, 53 (photo), 55

Backbone, 11–12
Badger (anatomy), 13 (artwork)
Balance (sense of), 26
Bat, 23 (photo)
    anatomy, 13 (artwork)
    echolocation, 23
    nose, 25
    speed of, 10
    See also Brown bat.
Bear, 30, 42, 47, 53
    See also Grizzly bear, Polar bear.
Beaver, 24, 33, 42
Black rhinoceros, 6 (photo)
Blood, 38–39
Blue whale
    anatomy, 8–9 (artwork), 10
    eating habits, 34
    endangerment of, 55
Brain, 15–16
Breast-feeding, 14 (photo), 46–47
Breathing. *See* Respiration.
Breeding. *See* Mating.
Brown bat, 55
Buffalo, 47
    See also Water Buffalo.

California gray whale, 52
California ground squirrel, 30
Camel, 15, 21 (photo), 35
Camouflage, 52, 53
Carbon dioxide, 4–5, 38, 39, 44

Carnivore, 30
Cat
    anatomy, 11 (artwork), 15
    eyesight, 21
    hearing, 22–23
    as a pet, 54
    scent glands, 24
    young of, 46, 47
Cattle, 54
Cheetah, 9–10, 10 (photo)
Chimpanzee, 40 (photo)
Chipmunk, 42, 53
Commerson's dolphin, 46
Cow, 35, 45 (artwork)
    See also Cattle.
Coyote, 24

Deer, 24, 35, 47
Deoxyribonucleic acid (DNA), 5
Diet, 30–34
Digestion, 30, 34–36
Dog
    hearing, 22–23
    as a pet, 54 (photo)
    sense of smell, 24
    young of, 46
Dolphin, 24, 47, 54 (photo)
    See also Commerson's dolphin, Striped
      dolphin.
Duck-billed platypus, 43 (photo)

Ears. *See* Hearing.
Echolocation, 23–24
Egg development, 42–44, 46
Egg-laying mammal. *See* Monotreme.
Elephant
    babies (calves), 47
    brain, 15
    defense, 54
    drinking habits, 34
    ears, 22
    gestation period, 46
    nose, 25
    See also African elephant.